APPALACHIAN SPRING

APPALACHIAN SPRING

New & Selected Poems

KATHLEEN M. SEWALK

Introduction by Guicang Li

TUNNEL PRESS, LTD.

2014

FOR CATALOGING AND INTERNET SEARCH DATA
Sewalk, Kathleen M., 1952-
Appalachian spring: new and selected poems
168 pp.
Includes index and glossary
ISBN 978-0-941461-11-5 hardcover w/ dust jacket
1. Appalachia   2. Pennsylvania   3. coal and steel heritage   4. women's literature
5. new age spirituality   5. poetry organic verse   6. haiku

Book design by Troy Scott Parker, Cimarron Design, Boulder, Colorado

Tunnel Press, Ltd.
3589 Menoher Boulevard, Suite 100
Johnstown, Pennsylvania 15905

Printed and bound in the United States of America

To Sogyal Rinpoche for giving
us the comfort of Buddhist wisdom
as we learn the dance of dying and living,
and for our parents who take us to the dance.

before enlightenment, chop wood, carry water
after enlightenment, chop wood, carry water

Contents

Acknowledgements

MANY INFLUENCES, FRIENDLY and not, impact an artist's life through its learning, growing, gestation, and creation cycles. Cycles of taking and of learning how to receive. Cycles of living with Spirit and of living without it. Cycles of ignoring nature, of discovering the God that is in all sentient beings, and of co-creating with Nature. Cycles of health and of infirmity. Cycles of being the child and parenting parents. Cycles of loving and of leaving. Cycles of living in a duality of absolute black and white and of living in the continuum of gray. Cycles with children and with being childless. Cycles of imposed medicine and of being responsible for self healing. Cycles of being nurtured and of facilitating healing in others. Cycles of Western arrogance and of Eastern humility. Cycles of Christian dogma and of ancient mysteries and ageless wisdom. To the teachers who cultivated these blossoms in my life and to those whom I now teach, I honor you and thank you for our time to grow together in respect and fond memory.

To Catherine Blake at Tunnel Press, Ltd. who chooses to print this book. To early mentors, Robert Francis, Denise Levertov, and Ruth Whitman. To Joseph Campbell and Robert Bly for lighting the fire that never dies. To Martha Murphy, Rick Page, Mike Karcher, Park Cover, and Suzette Johnson who understand my sensibilities and have collaborated with me in my mixed media projects for decades.

To Chester and Stella Sewalk, our parents married for 76 years who taught us love, reconciliation, forgiveness, and patience. To my families—past, present and future whose lessons have shaped what I am. To lifelong friends and colleagues who tolerate my demands and humor me. To my pets who give unconditional love. And to my garden, healing teachers, angels, guides, and elementals of the natural world who deliver unceasing healing energy, Beauty and Joy to my days. To all, accept my humble and eternal gratitude for the journey.

Kate Sewalk

Foreword

Tunnel Press, Ltd. celebrates its 40th year as an independent publisher which began as a small press serving the literary community of the consortium of colleges in Worcester, Massachusetts. Professors, adjunct faculty, and the Worcester County Poetry Association mentored its early publications and endeavors. *GOB: A Poetry Magazine* featured student and faculty work from Assumption College, Clark University, Worcester Polytechnic, and Holy Cross. The state government and college literature departments fostered mentorships, readings and seminars by master poets Robert Bly, Denise Levertov, Robert Francis, Sonia Sanchez, and Ruth Whitman, to name a few. Several of these beloved mentors are infirm or have since passed but their legacy lives on. They fueled the fire to forge organic musical form in poetry and gave voice to a group of poets, Kate Sewalk being among them, who are still working and who, in turn, have mentored two generations of younger writers since then. Much in publishing and in schools has been sustained through the vision and funding in those early years by the National Endowment for the Arts and state groups such as the Massachusetts and Pennsylvania Poets and Artists in the Schools programs. What began with poetry writing residencies has grown to include fiction, non-fiction, dance, music, art, metalwork, pottery, and many genres of creative expression.

During our early years, when printing with offset lithography we consumed vast amounts and tonnage of paper. Our social responsibility to the environment has been demonstrated with our reforestation efforts in the Androscoggin Basin of Maine in cooperation with Boise Cascade. Our trees will be harvestable beginning 2017 and afterward.

Our commitment to the ideals of the small independent press movement have remained constant. Following our relocation to Pennsylvania, our titles continue to have a focus on regional interests particular to Pennsylvania, the farming, coal and steel heritage of its people, its artists, and its writers who chronicle the passion and fervor of this landscape and history. Our commercial retail imprint has offered women's and New Age titles in keeping with our mission of advancing the self sufficiency and independence of women and promoting the writings and thoughts of an ageless wisdom. Our Legacy Editions™ imprint features private commissioned limited edition titles written to chronicle the stories of influential families in the region who created an indelible mark on the history of the area. *The Cutting Edge* (the story of ASKO the American Shear Knife Company of Pittsburgh), and *The Story of Rolling Rock* record the influence of the Benjamin Rackoff and Richard King Mellon families, respectively. *After the Storm* anthologizes, through poetry and non-fiction, the experience of the Johnstown Flood of 1977. Our Legacy Edition™ art books and private commission works are beautifully crafted, letterpress printed on archival papers and hand bound in limited editions. *Singing of Fruit* showcases the literary tradition of haiku and is graced with the characters of Chinese translations by Guicang Li and Japanese translations by Mineo Moritani. Somerset County artist Martha Murphy illustrated the edition and watercolored the relief etchings and art on every page.

This is the tradition which brings us to this year's offering. *Appalachian Spring* embodies the essence of our 40 years as an independent small press publisher. With it we carry on our celebration of women's literature with Sewalk's collection of poems. We acknowledge the original works in which these poems have appeared. Most satisfying for us is that the printed book is as beautiful, hearty and long-lasting as its poetry. We thank our long-time collaborator Troy Scott Parker at Cimarron Design for making it beautiful and organic in every way. We thank Dustin Greene for audio production of the poetry readings Sewalk prepared for naturalist, women's, and New Age audiences. The compact disc of this collection of live readings is bound and boxed in a private custom binding of this volume of her collected works.

In the tradition of a colophon we offer and honor this retail title in this manner. *Appalachian Spring* is set in Adobe Jenson Pro, an historic revival capturing the essence, strength, and beauty of two icons of Renaissance type, Nicolas Jenson's roman and Ludovico degli Arrighi's italic. It is printed in an edition of 300 copies on non-acid, non-recycled paper. The binding is Smythe sewn, covered in cloth over boards, foil stamped, and bound in a three-piece

Western style case. The book is accompanied with a four-color printed and laminated dust jacket. Twenty copies are offered with clamshell conservation boxes foil stamped in gold with leather labels. The edition is a rarity in this age of commercial trade printing of poetry. The excitement of superior book making is matched by the world of *Appalachian Spring* which is exciting in its representation of the coal and steel heritage of the area, the richness of the Appalachian woodlands, the lives of the women who live there, their dreams, and spiritual growth to embrace ideas well beyond this sacred landscape.

Catherine Blake
July 2013

Introduction

WHEN I SERVED as a faculty member at the Critical Languages Department at Indiana University, Tunnel Press approached me to translate a collection of haiku into Chinese. [The original art book publication of *Singing of Fruit*, which appears here on pp. 92-95.] They also commissioned a Japanese translator to do the same. Out of curiosity, I agreed to give it a try, for I didn't have any idea how well an American poet would handle this particularly challenging oriental poetic form. So impressed by its startlingly beautiful lines after I read the first few, I couldn't stop reading them all until I finished the collection. There are a number of poems of Kate's that I turn to again and again.

I have read haiku poetry in translation. A highly compressed form of Japanese poetry, a haiku usually consists of seventeen syllables, commonly divided among three lines in a pattern of 5-7-5. Because of its length limit, brevity is the core of a haiku. Brief as it is, it narrates a story or presents a vivid picture in a style as is prevailing in the oriental line painting, leaving the reader to draw out the details to complete in the mind's eye.

Dichotomy is often hidden in a haiku. And experienced haiku poets enjoy playing with the dualism of the dialectics of Yin and Yang, which often take such fairly specific forms as in the near and the far, foreground and background, past and present, present and future, day and night, mobility and immobility, the high and the low, the solemn and the lively, sound and silence, temporality and eternity, etc. Similarly, experienced readers get a tremendous amount of pleasure from the witty interplay of dichotomy and the dualism of Yin and Yang.

Most of Kate's poems work on the dynamics of such a dualism. And they work amazingly well. Take the first poem for example, snow clings to the rock, ready to *"race the run off."* A perfect interaction of immobility and mobility is activated in just four words. Philosophy, feelings, understanding, appreciation, and imagery integrate into a totality of all. It is also an image fraught with personal experience, thus it gives meaning to experience.

What characterizes Kate's haiku poetry is its profound seriousness and the almost heroic idealism, reminiscent of John Keats, Rainer Rilke, William Carlos Williams, and Theodore Roethke. By this, I mean there is always a presence in her poetry of a search for wisdom and understanding—mingled with a slight sadness, yes, a slightly sad search, as embodied in *"Gifts lie in the letting go / without fear or care / Sheep shearing in March."* Here sadness blends with a strong optimism in moving on, in embracing life. Quite a few poems in this collection express similar sentiments as in the haiku about the lone pony, and the sparrows in the snow-bound places.

Kate's poetry is a means to extend her willingness to let sublime spirituality enter her field of concentration and take over a devotion to the sublime and ideal. This is achieved through her unique perception of light, which is used as an exclusive synecdoche for spirit infusing meaning. Many poems emit a phosphorescent glow. Through light, the ordinary becomes extraordinary, and the trivial becomes significant.

Many poems are my favorites. Natural and esthetic experiences are mutually transposed in *"Row turns upon row / teams of draught horses rut the fields / Seed spirits rise in the air."* The complexity of human relationships is afforded due in such simple physical reality as *"Separate oak limbs / even touch and bend together / to weather a storm."* A smooth relationship suddenly gets taut and ends nowhere as in *"She dreamed him into her life / The avalanche now in her heart / love with nowhere to go."* The intensity of the tragic operates an esthetic catharsis in us all. And paradoxical perceptions are explored in the rhythmic interplay of word, image, wisdom, idea, and feeling in *"Joy is not in the walking / but awakening / in the silence there."* Each philosophically synthesizes into the other, stimulating change from "walking" to "awakening" and to "silence," a higher level of understanding and ideal. Her ingenious way of presenting the harvest season of autumn strikes me the most. It is common to present autumn from the visual or the auditory perspective, but Kate sings of autumn from her olfactory sensibility, *"August smells rush forth / piercing the nose while flies buzz / Silage fermenting."* All of a sudden, autumn transcends and we humans transmute. We are part of the harvest season, and autumn, is a part of us.

At that time of my original translation of *Singing of Fruit* I celebrated Kate's brilliant collection of haiku poems and felt in the presence of a true zen spirit.

REVIEWING THE GROUP OF POEMS FOR THIS COLLECTION, one traces the growth of this zen spirit. *Singing of Fruit* can now be seen in the context of this larger journey; centered in the middle of the collection it is the bridge between the real and the spiritual.

The seven chapters walk the ascending path of man's human journey on a spiritual quest to link with the Divine. Affirmation of similar steps in Jewish, agnostic, Christian and Buddhist mysticism are found throughout and give testament to the poet's internalization and understanding of the unity among spiritual traditions—all are one. Translations from the *Tao te Ching* that introduce the chapters reflect ageless wisdom and serve as a river that winds through the collection, connecting it, flowing with it, defining it, and taking it to its Source.

The poet's journey begins with the poetry affirming the author's roots in the coal fields of Appalachia and baptism into her eastern European tribe. The history of communion and relationships, sexuality, marriage, loves and losses follows. Third is the awareness and definition of the self in the many facets and aspects of womanhood. The universal human experience of *suffering, love and compassion* in the fourth chapter connects the poet to all humanity with an ability to love beyond the self through the suffering of others. This is captured in the epic struggle of holding on to life and waiting for death in poems selected from a 10-year collection, "Conversations with Stella." Communication with Nature becomes the poet's portal to the eternal gift and hope of life in the fifth chapter. Living in the physical world and awakening to the zen of Spirit within the physical are the essence of the sixth chapter. The collection completes itself full circle with selections from *Three Months on the Mountain*. In these poems we find the poet's vision quest that retraces her journey. It culminates in the awakening of the poet's realization and connection to the Divine and eternal.

As seen in *Singing of Fruit*, each chapter philosophically synthesizes into the other, stimulating change from "walking" to "awakening" to a higher level of understanding and ideal that is found in *Appalachian Spring* as a whole.

Guicang Li, Ph.D.
Professor of English
Dean of the College of International Education
Zhejiang Normal University
Jinhua, Zhejiang, China

I

From
Past the Conemaugh Yards

Everything must have its roots
to grow and flower and flow.

Return to your roots
learn simplicity; it is all you need to know.

PAST THE CONEMAUGH YARDS

for David McCullough

I
Johnstown
in southwestern Pennsylvania
lies in the mountains
on a nearly level flood plain
at the confluence of two rivers
at the bottom of an enormous hole in the Alleghenies
as though the bottom dropped out
leaving it angry and smoldering.
Mills sit below town
in a gap in the mountains
where the Conemaugh flows westward.
The valley
full of smoke
going night and day.

On hillsides trees turn an evil-looking black;
grow no leaves.
Downstream from town
the rivers,
stained
by waste dumped from the mills.
Acrid smells
and loud stink prevails.
Mill workers
fight dirt daily,
saving every spare nickel.
Miners and strapping steel workers,
with an energy
a vitality to life
are rough and busy with the rush
of quaking mills.

With thick black mustaches
and beards,
limping down from the Blue and White buses
at the Gautier
or at Bethlehem's portals
with their silver lunch buckets
waiting for the shift
to change—
      daylight,
      second turn,
      and hoot owl.
Success and fortune in the entire valley
depends nonetheless
on how red those skies glow at night.

When furnace doors open
great tongues of flame
shoot up in the pall around Johnstown.

The open hearths
great places of vague human forms,
heavy labors
and dancing fires.

Red skies on the mountain
seen from Ehrenfeld and South Fork
remembered by Schwab
Carnegie, Frick and the others—

"It gets into your hair,
your clothes,
even your blood."

II

On the hillsides
of Cambria County
halfway between Johnstown
and the crest of the Allegheny range,
ran the throb of perpetually passing trains
past the Conemaugh yards.
Giant hemlocks, oaks,
hickories, black birch and silver maple
grew along densely forested ridges.
In spring
there was superb fishing
along the Conemaugh and Stonycreek,
above the town the water ran clear
full of mullet, catfish, eels,
walleyed pike, trout, sunfish
and swift, mud-colored crayfish.
In the fall
when the sorghums
turned blood red against the pines,
there was great hunting on the mountain.
Black bear and wildcats on Laurel Hill;
eagles were spotted overhead.
There were pheasants, ruffed grouse,
geese and loons;
wild turkeys up to twenty pounds.
Panthers and passenger pigeons
scattered across the valley.
In winter
there were sleigh rides to Ebensburg
and many nights
were the way mountain nights were meant to be;
air better than man could ask for;
with millions of stars overhead,
in a sky the color of coal.

WOMAN TRACKS, BARONS AND COWHERDS

I
Even as she walks, tracking past the frozen pastures;
coal yards outside town, the snows in deep January
push her back. Legs and calves stiffen in the silent weight.

She moves home, by the coal tipple, the smell of wood smoke
lumbers, in stacks, from the chimneys of row houses.
All traces of her face fade as steam from her mouth trails
                                in the pale air.

She is a peasant woman from central Poland, one
of many who came to America to be widows,
in Pennsylvania; serfs in the soft coal fields.

Winters have been the same since she left the innocent
hut, outside St. Florian's Gate in Krakow, her legs
wrapped in a thin coat; with dress down to her ankles.
                        As a young girl,

she left to work for bread and promises. Traveling
to the estates of barons, the *szchlactas* of Poland.
There she dug potatoes and red cabbage, on road farms

from Mietkov to Ksiazenice, from Sunday to Sunday.
Through the years she watched the snow come, china white and clean.
like silk bedsheets and French dresses, pressed and polished;
                        baron perfect.

And when the ice came, she wore her winter feet, beet red
in scrawny fur-trimmed galoshes. Over covered fields
she pulled dumb innocent cows from the storm to the barn,

the bruises inside her girlish thighs trudging through snow.
These were the legs given to barons
these were the legs given to cowherds.
                              And her body

changed. She made it dance to the rhythm of blood and sperm;
all for a wool coat with buttons from the mills near Poznan,
for new stockings, and the promise of America.

II
Here her tracks have been firm and long; they leave and arrive
where men once came inside. Through streets in the mining town
she peddles knit handiworks, quilts, baked pastries from her
                              empty kitchen;

selling wares to supplement each day. Remembering
grease and orange sulphur on his wet clothing after the night shift,
in the mud below the drift; his rubber knee pads worn through;

each morning, delicately wiping coal from his eyes
with vaseline and embroidered kerchief, and his silver
bucket that always came back to the kitchen, except
                              on that last day.

Even as she walks, tracking past the frozen pastures
toward home, she passes drops of blood in the white snow,
marking the broken legs of a small bird caught in the branches.

And further on, his name on the mailbox, waiting
to give her benefits each week with the Union check;
always pushing her back; her legs stiff from the silent weight.

THE BOAT MEN

From under a tundra moon
yellow and round with promise
hearty boys fled the Ukraine
left the borscht, the bulgar and buckwheat,
fled the armies of Franz Joseph
before the Revolution ended the czars
allowing hope and meat for the poor.

While their mothers wept over rosaries
on pilgrimages
to the Black Madonna in Czestochowa,
they traveled north
to battered ships in the Baltic
with nothing but gypsy memories,
strong backs, wild music, and songs
a pocket full of dancing tongues
        Polish, Hungarian,
        Slavish, Ukranian,
they could dream in any language.

In Gdansk, Gydnia and Kaliningrad
boys were bounty for the boat men
paid $5 by industrialists
for each pair of beet red hands sent to America
bound for Baltimore
years before the welcome
of Ellis Island and Lady Liberty.

They came to carry water and feed mules
in the mines of Shamokin and Wilkes-Barre
Pennsylvania anthracite towns;
in Cassandra, Portage and Lilly
soft coal company towns.

In lives lit by carbide and canaries
they learned to pick coal
and build dingy frame duplexes
painted black with soot from boney piles;
yellow with sulphur from the mills.
They bought and paid for life at the company store
earning new dreams 16 tons at a time.

From them, a legacy of generations
capable of work, capable of the world;
Cossack stubborn and mazurka proud
      miners, musicians, mechanics,
      farmers, writers, and artists,
      doctors, cooks, and waiters,
      lawyers, chemists, and furriers,
      designers and equestrians
each self-confident like the rhythms
of the fiddle and the string bass.
They dance through life
with the passion and zest of the steppe
with gusto and fire in their eyes
a kick of the heels
and a *czardasz* in the heart.

EARTHWORMS

Winter has kept them
in an underground climate
a comfortable sixty degrees.

Work and the need to eat
keeps them
        warm;
sustains life
and keeps their bodies
          pliable.

The frost line comes deeper
drives them,
pushes harder, farther;

they make a way downward
with all their moving parts—
tiny particles in the earth
some theory in a Newtonian universe.

Cool black earth
passes through their veins
as they dig tunnels and entryways

they pass layer upon layer
left somewhere as human memory;
sediment and organic waste
old as the Babylon of Nebuchadnezzar
or older remnants of a Pennsylvanian period.

They pierce a soft coal layer
and burrow through like moles
as they have done for centuries—
continuous bituminous miners.

And on wet mornings
smelling damp
like roots and bulbs passed
on their way up to the showers,

they hurry out of their holes
carrying the dirt home with them;
bringing their gritty mouths up into the air.

FOSSILS

for Joe Mehora Sr., Mine Operator 8-South
Cambria Division, Bethlehem Mines, December 4, 1972

The Appalachian Mountains
are from another period
Pennsylvanian   Cambrian.

Inside them
fossil ferns
and the soft prints of sandpipers
lie seamed in coal

without sound;
without air
waiting to rise out of the mountains.

Miners from Ehrenfeld, South Fork and Mineral Point
towns built on the edges of "boney piles"
come to work in the Bethlehem Mines,
at Brookdale, 8-South, and Cambria Slope.

They dig in tunnels and shafts
working the coal,
bringing the fossils up

to the open spaces
where light has come to the vein.

Under pressure
the coal companies
create newer fossils
to be unearthed from rock falls
at a later time, with later work orders.

The broken shoulders, twisted limbs,
spines and fingernails of crushed miners
have been doubled over like bent leaves
under new weight
when the roofs collapse.

In tight seams
these men lie still; waiting to surface
to the open spaces
where light comes to the vein.

They are leaving a mark
in the wash house, in the drift, at home,
and in the dark places with holy sounding names
  Bethlehem   Bethlehem

without sound
without air
spirits waiting to rise out of the mountains.

DUENDE

*"all that has dark sounds has duende…it does
not appear if it sees no possibility of death…"*
– Federico Garcia Lorca

At this window
there is a presence
that moves easily through

curtains,   sheer,
it moves as melancholy moves,

from some deep heavy place
solidly it turns
        out
and under again;

carries the smell
of damp and musty cellars.

It is with the miner;
his silver lunch bucket
coming home to the kitchen;
in the clothes dirt,
        black
slicks around his eyes,
and in the spaces of the skin
where his sweat lives.

This presence carries his children
        back
in the summer

when they'd sleep out
in abandoned mountain caves
deep
        on black beds,

where they were heavy
and dreams told them
they too

        will be turning
between the cool veins of coal
cramped, like the bones of their fathers.

BENEATH THE HOUSE

…there is a charm among old Russian women
which promises that if they rub certain
rocks found along the edge of the river
and do a ritual dance, they will bring life and good
fortune to their families…

I
This town is an acid river place,
its children and waters
have been where the mines are

running through coal towns
underground
where, earth, air

time and women
all smell used and old;
their noises dark

empty
          to the men
beneath the house.

Only the sulphured rocks in the river
are warm, orange
their small acid-eaten pores
let time out.

II
In shifts
the men go under
to work in the Cambria County coal mines
at Ehrenfeld and Fiffick Town.

Their wives and children wait;
daily along the sulphur river,
and at night the company houses

now with toilets and aluminum siding,
are open: the women alone.

The dark walls in empty houses
leave no corners
to hide in.

Through cool cellars
dripping with green,
the women go down to the streams

to where they are
washers of river rock
in the waters
beside the house.

III
The starched old Russian women
in stiff dresses scrub the rocks
polishing wildly with knuckled fingers;
in circles
        times three
erasing the scum
erasing the sin
from the orange rock

twirling, swirling
with dress hems wet in the water
like crazed gypsies in a magic dance.

IV
As the whistle blows
at the mine portal
the night shifts;
midnight dampness
pushes the women back home,
woman and stones
women and stone.

They run heavy breasted
and carry the stone legends with them
to tight houses and tense beds

with their secrets;
their rites.

They place the stones in
enameled coffers from the Ukraine
hidden under goose down pillows,

and they are waiting
for the whistle
waiting

for the miracle
to bring back life and love
to the hungry ones at home

waiting for the miners
in sunken caves
beneath the house

waiting for the loon,
green lilies and water weeds,
waiting for the men
with their silver buckets

to return from the black river
beneath the house.

THE AMISH COME TO SCHOOL

Carriage wheels whirr,
clatter to the brick school yard;
the horse is hitched to a chestnut tree.

Lucille and Noah Zimmerman, 18 and 20
shuttle three small girls to public school
in long skirts and cotton blue bonnets.

The parents are a well-bred team
brightly spirited and graceful
with high, healthy cheekbones
flushed as peaches in August.

Noah wears pot-cropped hair, thick;
slick as boot black.
limp like a mane from his head;
no sideburns under the Amish round hat.

Denim overhauls hang
suspended from barnlike shoulders
over a home-made cotton shirt.

His hands are clean
smooth as leather;
imaginative.

His woman carries
a sprinkle of freckles on her face
below eyes that are a field of light.

A spare dusting of ash
covers pointy high-top shoes
laced over saggy black wool stockings.

Wrapped in a floor-length dress
and gingham bonnet
she is a cotton blend of black and blue,
hand sewn from hem to crown.
She simmers in the summer heat.

Stiff pleats in her skirt
hide her curves;
give sound to her quiet figure.

She moves with the rustle
of wind blown grain
and is fertile as the earth they keep.

Hawkish country mothers
have also come to school with children
in the Martinsburg farm town.

They gab and stare
                awed
at the subtle mysteriousness of her sex

in the same way
they always stare at Zimmerman's General Store,
the Post Office and Saturday auctions in town.

They wonder
whether she wears hair on her legs;
and if babies have left sags in her belly.

They guess
how long her years are
tucked under the bonnet,
and if he strokes her at night
when her braids are down.

They imagine his hands
if he milks her breasts;
what it's like when he makes love to her,

how often they lay together
tilling the furrows between her legs
plowing and sowing in the acres of night,
and if she makes little noises in the dark.

Lucille and Noah
have learned to weather
these splashes of local color,

they carry their God with them
deep in the soft folds above her eyes
and under his wet boots
where the earth cakes.

RANDOM CREATURES

"Imitate the Spirit of the animal or the thing inside you."
– Salish

In October
the world is a circus
of buzzing creatures.
Soft skinned spiders

bring themselves in
clustered now;
hiding in tight underground spaces.

Their eyes
move reluctantly
in the daily blackness.

Squirrels
in red and grey
flop, limb to limb
along tree shafts.

They rustle forage
to underground caves
putting in their time.

The spirits
of underground creatures
all move

as men move
in and out of the coal mines
stockpiling timber
and little pieces of themselves.

DOWN THE MOUNTAIN

Another season begins;
the white hunters—
nabobs and muckamucks

garbed in orange fluorescent
outfit a new character,
            sketch
plots for stalking the whitetail.

Weeks of preparation
outlining the action;
brushing up their tall tales;

buying cartridge shells
toe warmers and arctic mittens;
long range scopes

to clarify their vision
and other novel items
for heroes on the hunt.

Polishing four-wheel drives
developing new relationships,
a good ole buddy with a big
            ten four.
Each trip out a new climax.

Year after year
they track a solution
to a larger chain of events,

finding the denouement in their vision.
With horns locked
and the scent of blood hot fur on their backs

they can be seen
dragging dead dear poems
down the mountain.

2

Everything has both yin and yang in it
and from their rise and full coupling comes new life.

.

DRIVING ACROSS PENNSYLVANIA

A late winter sun
blankets the fields
horses with muzzles nuzzled
and heads nodding for more;
Paints and Pintos
Roans and Appaloosas
dappled in color.

A black flock of geese
moving north from the Chesapeake
stopping by on their wing
to points North
pass over a staccato of arbor vitae
dotting fields and farms
furrows dreaming of winter wheat.

The Amish boy behind a team
of draught horses splits the fields
he dreams of walking through her blue gate
with flowers.

MAPS

He engineers the terrain
scales and sizes every contour
creating roads between them,
joining two places
that have been nowhere.

At night they are a map,
like Africa and South America
sleeping once side by side
and then slowly sliding apart
as she moves
to the far reaches of the bed,
an ocean between them.

It is the need to be free
that separates; sets boundaries.
Each fears the inevitable turn of history.
the endless motion of geography.

Each is a continent with its own
ring of fire.
He is Africa,
a blond Sahara with deep heat,
and she, Brazil,
a jungle darkness
pushing off from his side.

Listen to the sounds,
what you hear is a primal fire, feminine;
her faults are weak,
and the dark earth
beneath her ridges
carries such violent rumblings.

CHANSON IN A MINOR

If I could live
in eternal September
with its bounty full

if I could live
to only remember
Love with you

evergreen
like spruce and hemlock
strong and bending as they grow

then I would live
in eternal September
and rejoice in Beauty before the snow

for Love is
all there is
and all you'll ever need to know.

SPRING CLEANING

This is the ceremonial busk
Thoreau wrote about
when the Passamaquoddy Indians
burned every possession each Spring
in gratitude and grace for the past
consecrating a new future.

Today, April shouts
the small steps it takes towards summer
        with cocky rides in convertibles
retreat again on days of snow.

April shouts
for a new life, a new season.
It wants a reason to begin vivid promises
even the tulips are reluctant
to spread.

In the small house
the couple weeds their nest;
Spring cleaning
is an act of war
against the dusty sameness.

Gloom and resentment washed away
yellow stains on walls, ceilings, beds,
are layered memories of each month,
                each year
it has been the same;
each crevice in the window
                panes
of a soiled view of life, forced expectations;
these too are scrubbed,
for a Pine Sol clean fresh start.

Silent faces in the mirrors sing—
drumming like tribes
making the effort, willing to burn it all

there will be no more ruts
no traps, no more routines.
Let there be change!
Let there be new perfumes,
new clothes, new colors, new music!

April shouts
an invitation to dance
invent new dreams
invent new fantasies
invent new roads and maps to get there.
Come as you are. Dress casual.
Bring your own passion.

LETTING GO

for Joann Johnson

So Mrs. Johnson
this is how it must have been
when you let go
deciding to sell this house.
The broom you left in the corner for luck
won't sweep your broken life away.
It has collected webs with spiders,
soft soothsayers, wary in quiet corners.

This is how it must have been
that last summer in the house with him,
staring mirrors, glaring
making you face it at every glance
watching your body fade and wrinkle
your feet dripping in the tub
naked and vulnerable at last
from his inevitable affairs.

When the heart goes, nothing lingers.

The letting go must have been
dust and newspapers piling,
dishes and brown rings collecting in the sink.

How things must have collected—
the trash, mildew on the ceramic tile,
laundry, unpaid bills and liquor bottles
as you waited patiently
for the storm
            windows to come off
one hot July night when you needed
                the screens.

Even the vegetable garden was conquered
by weeds

everything growing in its own way
and knee high grass
still not tall enough to hide in.

The broom says
that once making the decision to launch
the letting go is easy
you carry the storm within you
ride the waves inside
furling the jib
steady at the helm
beating upwind
screaming Amen!

PHOTO FROM THE DARK ROOM

Waiting for it to develop took time no one had
a marriage pushed in the processing
the final image too thin.

A magician with film
you captured life;
made it stand still
to change, manipulate
and posterize
suiting whim or fancy.

There was a wife
now a memory in black and white
bits and pieces of a soul

      a pair of feet, one bare shoulder,
      a woman hoarding lobster in the bay,
      among asparagus fern
      on a leaky Victorian porch
      overlooking the river and mills in town.

There were brown spots on the photos, decay,
they began to show quite early and remained.

The mystery is clear now—
      not enough time
      it's all in the wash.

Now and forever
under the amber
remember an afterimage of the early days
let it linger in your eyes.

A photographer
starting from nothing
with cheap furniture

bought from a Jewish woman on Green Street
      Giertra Ertzabet   Giertra Ertzabet

photographer born in a closet,
in the dark you found life.
          A wife

was one more negative image
to dodge and burn,
one more face for the fixer.

IN THE LEAVING

As you leave, into the moon
tracking across the shadows
on this crisp night

Yom Kippur recants
atonement, mercy, forgiveness
to end the past and glimpse the future.

In the yellow of the October moon
I am no longer a coward
I am what's wrong with my world
I am all that is right and in between
with my world.

I am silenced by the power of silence
where the head settles its chaos
to find the beat of the heart
where the rhythms of life
fall like leaves.

Dazzle me now, watch me fall;
to whom will I be beautiful as I go?
As my heart grasps
the dark sound of your step across the frost.

PACKSADDLE RIDGE

for Don Davis

In another October in a forward time
when the harvest sends its blush to red
as we make our final season
when our legs can no longer bring us here
I'll remember this course with you
at Packsaddle Ridge
high above Keezletown Road
sitting in two Adirondack chairs
on the 16th hole
a bottle of Pebble Beach scotch between us
telling stories of our shots and drives
our sports cars, sinking 30-foot downhill putts
and glorious dreams of par golf

our memories soaring like two birds
gliding the thermals
over the Shenandoahs to West Virginia
shadows entwined
circling endlessly through time.

In some history yet to come
We will have lost independence, a race hard won
driving will be all but done.
The festive garlands of fire between us
will lose their color at night
our fireworks will be silent and white.

3

Like a lake the heart must be calm and quiet.

Be like water, never fight, it flows around without harm.

HARPSICHORD

The star that's brightest on Christmas Eve—
Stella, is up before dawn, lighting the tree
sipping her coffee by the fireplace;
she smiles at what's been done
and readies her heart for the day.

From candles left dripping on the mantle
bayberry fills the air;
in the warm room evergreen boughs droop
as balsam needles rustle to the oak floor.
Diamond and pearl secrets squeal
from tiny jewelry boxes tied to the tree.
Polished sterling graces her table of linen and lace;
stemware catches a glimmer of light from the tree;
in the cellar wine gently cools.

As she enters the kitchen
her heart is a harpsichord of laughter.
An aroma of cinnamon, apple and pumpkin pies
glides through the house like a boy on new skates.
Chopped celery and onions begin to simmer
in sage and rosemary ready to dress the turkey.
In the pantry she works the dough as she always has
her peasant shoulders large and round
from years with her fists in the bowl.
Her homemade bread bakes
a warm spread of hot buttered memories.

Her day is like so many others
the women of Kwanza and Chanukah
pounding the chapatti, the matzah
searching in the nights
and Festivals of Light
hope for their lives
finding it all in the same places—

in giggling eyes and messy faces
of little ones, of daughters, of sons come home;
then there is nothing left for them to knead
just all the joyous mouths to feed!

GREY WINTER POEM

Winter blows in wildly
                         again.
In December old women
remember when their hair fell
darker to their shoulders,
and their finger bones
made no noise with movement.

At holidays
these women bake tradition,
boiling pumpkins;
                   stuffing poultry;
they do not watch the snow
                  or its coldness
until the children leave
the heat and spice of their kitchens—

then the white steam
around the windowpanes
will have cleared and
grey winter
                   will blow in wildly again.

WHEN MEN ARE AWAY ON THE HUNT

for Mary Jane

The sun slips away
from the young country woman
in late Fall.

Her body has been covered
thighs and shoulders, dry

stuffed into flannel underwear,
                 chapped;
the small dark rings around her eyes
count each year it has been the same.

Her color has fallen, tan faded;
since October
the world has not seen the sweet voice of her legs.

As more darkness enters
days are shorter and cold,
                 nights unpredictable

like the last hours of the whitetail buck
during a new gaming season
          when men are away on the hunt.

She takes a chance;
eagerly she goes behind the shed
                 back to her roots;

in these primary ways
she dares to be like him.
She leaves the kitchen

and begins chopping wood—

wielding sledge to axe
in rhythms;
                    dancing
for the Spirit of the wood
                    to shake loose;

a dizzy power
blows through her trunk
to her head, screaming

her body willows
yielding to the exhilaration
of new freedom.

She is amazed at the wet release,
warm sweat comes
        a sap rising in her body

from deep in the hollow pit of her back
and between the arch where her legs branch;

from a full bushy body
once pruned by canning fruits and jellies;
diapers and dishes.

Awesome. She stands
                    shaking
limbs raised like a sunflower
much as if she had walked
                    bare breasted
into a swarm of bees in late August.

COOKING FOR ONE

for Jean D'Amico

Why can't I pop through the door
at five, alive!
Eager to don the apron
dazzle them dead
dancing in the kitchen
with tea balls swaying from my ears;
whisking over the linoleum
no dishes ever dirty;
nothing to clean up; no left overs.
Cuisine, Greek lamb,
oriental won tons,
baba ganouge so good
that Syrians from Pittsburgh
would line up at my door;
even the French would cry for my fries.

I want to love to cook,
with gusto
like an old Italian friend outside Boston
planting herbs in a New England country garden
or buying eggplant in Cambridge;
dashing in the kitchen
blending and simmering
feeding a co-op of thirty friends

    ratatouille, linguini, fettuccine,
    in huge earthen mixing bowls;
    a feast for the eyes
    with her laughing Italian heart.

    I want to know the olive oil
    toss the greens;
    sense when to add the lemon
    and when it's time for a touch
    of mint.

I want to love to cook
like old European mothers
from scratch, something from nothing,
flour and water; endlessly feeding families
stretching pasta and cabbage
from Sicily to Krakow.
Women with shoulders large and round
from years with fists in the bowl
up to their elbows in dough
      ravioli, pierogie
      European pillows
      making beds to win hearts and husbands.

I want to
skip and kick down the walk
crisp in the winter air
past the rhododendron and hearty red
dogwood berries
past the welcoming pineapple and tangerines
at the door.

Kiss the cook in her herb garden glory
nibble all the wicked smells there
      fish in tarragon, and party bread with basil
      rosemary chicken
      cheesecake with cherries
      chamomile brewing
      buttery brioche.

Come home to her with presents and pine
greet her sparkling eyes
and chocolate smile;
let the world be soft, succulent
and wonderful for a while!

PITTSBURGH SYMPHONY

Gateway sternwheelers paddle beyond
barges on the Mon. The subway stops
at Steel Plaza; while memories of
Grant Street trolleys linger on.

Clydesdales cart carriages
over cobblestones at Station Square
and a centuries-old Belgian block
roadway on Smallman Street
paves a path through time.

There aromatic smells in The Strip
echo through the cold December air—
marketplaces in memory
      London, Morocco, Genoa, Venice,
      Athens, Beijing, Honk Kong,

pretzels and chestnuts
steaming in the marketplace;
there are egg rolls and yakitori
      near Sambok's,
oranges and pomegranates
      from Aliotos.

Wholey's fish market
fillets a sea of flounder
still flapping and snapper still
        snapping,

while buckets of thick fish
chowder boil near barrels of
oyster crackers.

Flower vendors in top hats
hustle roses on Forbes;
students with portfolios
bustle through traffic.

Bright-eyed children with faces
chapped and cherry bright,
bundle up in scarves gazing

at treasures in holiday windows at
Macys, and uptown women
parade through Saks in sapphires and furs.

Holidays in the city—
Tchaikovsky's *Nutcracker* and ballerinas;
Handel welcomes the *Messiah* to St Paul's

Bach's Brandenburg concertos
spiral madly up columns and walls
glorious crescendos in grand concert halls.

A crisp staccato and quick *pizzicato*
of woodwinds and strings;
the *rallentando* a melancholy cello brings;
with trumpets charging the air
in quick rhythms of pomp and fanfare.

Men and women dressed to the nines
waltzing a joyous holiday pace—
their own fantasia in satin and lace.

A city with hearts to the sky. Fly
above the Angelus bells. Fly
above cathedral domes and spires of glass,
like tin angels over Mt. Washington,
                    hovering there;

catching the Spirit over the rivers, over
the bridges of night. Glowing where
love hides—in the dazzle; in the acres of light!

IN NO PARTICULAR ORDER

for Louise Beckley Varner

For men who write
life is a series of books
written every few years
on semester breaks and sabbaticals;
marked by grants and prizes
cocktail readings with caviar
and autograph parties for society ladies at tea;
no babies.

At sixty-one you letterpress the pages
of your first book
marked by aching back and ink black
fingers, page by page
laboring from love
as with your five children.
You are a "printer, writer, wife and mother,
in no particular order."

You say, "there are so many poems
left behind"
nothing is final.
So many lost letters
ems and ens and slugs
all the unassembled signatures
bits and pieces of furniture
never caught in the chase.

SO MANY POEMS

for Louise Beckley Varner

"There are so many poems
that are left behind"
fleeting images
like skipping ropes
quick lines
barely touching the concrete.

So many poems
like dark-haired little girls
women try to bear
to give meaning to life;
courting and skirting loves
in the sheets and pages
hoping to get caught.

These are the poems
that clutter minds forever
memories of all we have not done
like nymphs and gnomes
taunting all that's fine or evil
in our bones,
dreams and charms
we want to pen;
pencil a sketch of life with words.

We live a life of unmade poems
blending beds and babies;
poems are born by chance—
on the bus
a quick rendezvous at lunch
among computer reports at the office
or during the ever permanent press
of the laundry.

"For women to write"
is a dependent clause;

we must refuse commas
and thunder any pause that slows us down
we knead our poems with life
methodically punctuated with periods
capitalizing on all that's left behind there—
                    a rip, a tear,
                    a jag of the heart.

WRITER'S BLOCK

for Heather Campbell

The best cure for writer's block
find something or someone to edit
an old lover you want to change
verses to rearrange.

To affect this magic
one needs to clean house
a scavenger hunt

in every nook and cranny
dusty memories in crevices
like some dirty remodeling job left too long gone

finding poems on napkins, scraps of paper
scribbled like all writers do
quick images captured like fingerprints
    not to be lost or let go

stuffed away hiding everywhere
under this, under that
like dust bunnies.

Stuff them all into a piñata
blindfold yourself, spin furiously
wildly breaking it all open

eager in anticipation
cracking the bat
to finish one of these sweet treats!

COMING HOME

for Joan Karcher

1
Already
the apple pickers near Hancock
are pruning the brittle dead
from the fruitwoods;
waiting for sap to rise in the orchard.

2
Returning to the homestead
at Easter
there is an added fullness
each time the brothers come
home to mother.
They bring warm paschal foods
wrapped in white wicker baskets,
and their women
come to the pantry with apples and lilies,
carrying their firm ripe bellies
to the table.

3
In the kitchen they enter Spring
with a weathered mother
brewing coffee; baking fruit pies.
April branches above and below
as her heavy feet sway steadily among the babies
fragile saplings
clinging to her limbs like ivy.
Always
in the air around her, the pungent smells
of her husband—her tender
and keeper—
  her man who was constant in the past.
  The memories of his life

are pieces from her limbs
children, pruned and scattered
like small chips of bark
lying in little piles at her feet.

In this annual
repetition of fruits and life
mother is an orchard—
a door we all have to come through.

THE INSURRECTIONISTS

for Joan

The Pirates and Mets meet on the mound
spitting again; fair and foul;
the pitcher adjusts his hat, a rosin bag
his glove and shirt, his balls
things stick on sweaty August nights.

By the lamp posts along the streets
cicadas breathe in the air,
their cadences deep and steady
covered with tiny shells they raise shoulders
ready to rub their legs with sound.

In the long shadows of the street lights
a mailbox sits stuffed with poems
voices in darkness from women who write
about fathers and men, saints and lovers
in a world where liquor smells heavy
like thick slices of gin.

Some men seem to always be there for you—
Jesus, Maitreya Buddha and Muhammad
live in a condo down the street
but they're rarely home and don't leave a porch light on.
Bartenders are more friendly and don't ask you to change.

Here on this planet
St. Therese pilots a crew of women insurrectionists—
not Stepford wives who stay home making country crafts
not blonde amazons, 5'10" plus stiletto heels
with painted eyes like Egyptian concubines in orgasm;

but all the forgotten ones
working mothers, bankers and clerks
re-entering college at age 40
juggling kids, work, classes and PTA

the ones no one seeks
except for dinner and clean laundry
the discarded brunettes with gray hair
petite and only 5′2″ in boots
without photogenic high chiseled cheekbones
not television perfect
but with brains and hearts that won't quit
                              giving.

This crew of insurrectionists
marches in the summer night
leaving a trail of perfumed air.
They are a parade of strong and wicked hearts
zealots of passion
intense, hot to touch
with much at stake
dying to make a statement
like St. Joan yearning
for intimate satisfaction
in the heat and final fire.

FOR ALL THE NUBIAN WOMEN

The piercing Blacks
on the covers of *National Geographic*
at home in the deep heat of Africa
with red lips and painted faces
and jewels adorning necks and noses.

They stride, fearless and bare breasted
a perfect balance of power
carrying baskets.
To elevate them
photographers squat;
this low angle
never reveals their burden.

Look again closely,
see what women choose to carry
      books, food, and dirty laundry,
      plates, tools, and type from the foundry,
      computer reports, paint, and glue,
      cameras, guns, and dancing shoes.

Eskimos, Asians and Nubians,
Lapps, Amazons and Indians,
American women never seem to make the covers.

Women carry the world upright
stately on their head
balancing the load
with their babies in a sack

notice how they
never look down;
never look back.

VOTIVE

1

She plants two of each in her garden
only one heart in the house.
In the office he bows and dies daily;
at the lake he tells fish stories to live on.

Inside the stainless steel hospital
the woman lies amputated,
zapped and methodically poisoned;
her cut breast discarded on the floor
evermore without touch or caress
like a soldier at Gettysburg.

2

Burn the candles. Jingle the bells. Pray the Mass.
Gently dust off her broken heart,
for her quiet carpenter will return
with a smile and a hammer in his hand
bringing more Joy and Love
than she has ever known before.

The death eaters
keeping watch at the window
with hearts pounding
ready in a flurry at the door;
keeping the gate open—
so when she runs to greet Him down the walk
there'll be no fumbling with the lock.

3

Life teeters
like a solitary votive candle.
People brush by with their life—
passing quickly near
with a breeze of open air,

the flame burns wide and fast.
But mostly it burns a slow and definite
blue—hot and silent
alone in the alcoves.

RESTRINGING THE CELLO

The music stand in the loft lies silent
too many seasons without song
like birds flown South to winter
we will not winter another winter
without the melancholy dance
of strings.

Next year there will only be music
like cardinals at the feeder
a vibrato of red
in the crescendo of life.

MUSHROOMS

1

They are like peasant women
on the steppes of central Russia,
delicate flavors
to be mingled in ancient recipes.
Their plump gradual curves
are spotted with brown, fertile,
resilient with age and weather.
They carry private histories
clustered to the earth
tucked in narrow pockets under their caps.

We are hungry gypsies
amid the musk scents of the forest,
kneeling among the beech and rotted stumps,
picking wicker baskets full.
With our noses down in the moss dampness
we taste the moist heads
feed on the magic
and chance the poison.

2

The Earth Mother lies in quiet
full breasts open to the stars
her hips are full and round
like the ancients
soon her nipples will harden
with the breeze as it chills;
cicadas stop

> *Bats, cats and howling dogs*
> *spirits dance above burning logs.*
> *Blue moon, full moon, Hallows moon*
> *out with the witch; in with the fairy queen*
> *Teeth Mother, Earth Mother, dance alone,*
> *in the wisdom time of the goddess crone.*

AT BARBOURSVILLE

for Luca Paschina

Across the horizon, the mountains recline,
steel blue sleeping like a woman,
Earth Mother, with peaked breasts
rising high above a belly, rolling in gentle folds,
sloping to heavy thighs.

The heavy rain filled sky bears down like a lover
over the thin white sheet of dawn that covers her
a gray fog rises steaming in
from deep between the ridges.
At her feet, the Piedmont stretches before her.

This Earth Mother, is a landscape
from some ancient archaeology, a fertile valley.
At the foot of the mountain the Shenandoah winds
vineyards stripe the land
grapes, glowing fleshy and fragrant
        nebbiolo, sangiovese, cabernet franc,
        merlot, petit verdot, moscato, sauvignon blanc.

Layer upon layer a symphony of taste and fragrance
supple, lingering, round and radiant
sweet blush, crisp and fruity
a courtship of sun and rain
work of the hand, kiss of the land
sweet dance of the mountains,
at Barboursville, beyond the Ruins.

4

From
Sleeping Under the Rain

If no one wants anything for themselves
then there can be peace

and all things will know peace
the way music ends in peace.

MRS. GREEN

At 101, the woman in the next hospital bed
forecasts life 10 years into the future
thin, hollow, no visitors to notice
like a tree with creaking limbs
snapping, aging towards death
wild like a Doberman, snarling,
gnarling in raving pain
broken bones punctuated in endless groans
ohm   ohm   ohm

Mrs. Green cries out like an Evangelist,
      "Oh Jesus! Take me my sweet Jesus.
      Take me home. Just take me!"

      "I can't hear you
      Jesus my hearing aids are in the ER!
      Jesus my teeth are in the MRI!
      My Jesus, where are you?"

The nurse bellows, "Jezis be in another room
dahn the hall; He makin' his way to you, Honey."

      "Oh sweet Jesus. I'm so sorry; I'm so old and cranky
      I'm so very cold—from the inside.
      Oh, I have to pee. Jesus. Someone.
      Oh, it is warm, thank you thank you, Jesus.
      I am going back home with you today."

Here Jesus is a warm moment frozen in time.
At the sink on the other side of the curtain
I scrub, lather, scrub, lather;
the babbling cries for Jesus
      to walk on water across the room
are an infection I cannot wash off.

ODYSSEY

for our parents

I captain this wooden ship
on a downwind run
to the inevitable.

On this voyage I cannot tack
to make the journey longer;
or come about to reverse the course.

My crew teeters
defiant, reckless and resistant
screaming in the wind
      like two aged masts
bent and weakened
from endless rage with this storm.

They are spinning out of control
on a final Odyssey
into the vicious whirlpool of death.

Steady at the helm
I hold the rudder firm
watching these masts
splinter day-by-day

at the final moment
like Hercules at the Helispont
I will straddle this raging Hell for them
scoop them out of their spent bodies

scoop them into the gentle palms of my hands
and I will hurl them up
hurl them over the tides of life

in an alchemy of Love
I will hurl them like cosmic dust

beyond constellations
hurl them beyond the Milky Way
hurl them beyond all galaxies
where angels rest and play;
I will hurl them
into the calm black center of the Universe

where the Bible, Qu'ran, and the Bhagavad-Gita
     are one
where all great books
converge in a Word;
into the vortex of the absolute
I will hurl them
     a fleck of existence into eternity

with their souls fully awakened
thirsty to taste Illumination on
the blood red tongue of God.

THE WITHERING TIME

The couple is hit hard
as January delivers a chill.
He thinks it has been like this for months;
she is no longer the love he once knew.

Day by day he attends to her
beckoning call
        laundry, cooking,
        shopping, cleaning
building a road through the drifts that separate them.

Making a way through for some small compliment
some small acknowledgement
some small respect for his sacrifice
some small thank you
some small smile
to make it through this
winter that blows between them.

Day after day she does not notice
swears and glares quizzically
with a carnival grin of a mimed joker.

She cajoles him "What?"
        "Do you ever do anything for me?!"
Daily he watches his idea of her fade
like a spent flower
preserved only in his mind
fragile now—too long left in some old book
pressed only in his mind
flat and colorless
a small thinning shape
with a hint of color remaining
but without a soul behind her eyes.

This is her withering time after ninety winters
coming on full bore like a blizzard in January

each day she is drifting
in chill, in madness, in confusion.
Each day he shovels a new way through
        to gratitude
praying for the promise of a Spring
that may not come.

FROST

The first snow clouds of winter
roll back over the meadow, covering the sunset.

White rays of sun stream down over the Ridge
recalling some Biblical Transfiguration
when bodies crossed over to Heaven—

    for weeks the flowers have been thinning
    limbs are bent, losing their color; growing pale
    blossoms long gone, fallen
    petals like brown memories at their feet—
        the frost is coming, the frost is coming

    awesome anticipation and wonder
    long after they've gone to seed
    wild and reckless on the wind

    one small petunia, frail
    wraps around a hearty red dahlia
    curled alone under the moon waiting—
        the frost is coming, the frost is coming

    thin, spindly, drooping
    a sunken measure of her former beauty
    waiting for the last slump into white Light

    no more feeding or watering
    after the ebb and flow of good days and bad
    sun and rain, smiles and pain

aging parents on a journey beyond
waiting in this great in between time;
Knowing will come—cold and hard overnight
into a final morning.

CONVERSATIONS WITH STELLA

1

A scrawny Polish girl
scrubbing, sweeping, cleaning
soot, oily and black, high above the Bessemer mills in Franklin

her fingers raw like pink shrimp
timid sooty cinder girl
Cinderella finally recognizing her Prince.

Stella and Chester
95 and 97 years this time
75 years together in syncopated rhyme
                              living

through babushka mothers and bootlegger fathers
        moon shining corn liquor in secret batches;

through Sundays for courting lovers
dressed in spats, high heels and velvet suits
on walks past the Conemaugh rail yards
up the Mainline tracks to the Staplebend Tunnel

through banks closing, UMWA union strikes
        for the miner's wife
        and the Depression that never ends;

through *"sickness*
and health
'till death do us part"
the vow of the Greatest Generation

whose women had no choice
but pretend it was a fairy tale
moving through marriage beds and babies

striking at every chance
seeking the sweet spot of the marriage

always and ever needing more.

After the stroke and in her dementia;
it is her tale come home at last—
a prince to protect her

feed, bathe, and clothe her
she allows the Prince in him
only because *he makes it so*

for her, his vows
        only for her

                "in sickness
                and health,
                'till death do us part"

his one and only since grade school
        mating for life
                like cardinals

she the shabby insecure bird
he the showy confident male
the provider

who could make anything
        with work
her man, *her* Prince,

owned like rich jewels
hoarded in coffers
who *all* the girls in Franklin wanted.

2

My earth mother says,
after a stroke in the night,
    "Everyone in our family dies in October.
    Why is that you think?"

She pauses one stroke before the midnight
of her living, Cinderella at the pumpkin stage
anxious for life to go back to what it was.

I inhale;
hold her breath in my heart
lungs bursting not to let it go, her child lost and drowning.

At home in my forest along Laurel Ridge,
the melancholy call of a barn owl
splits the night before sunrise

this Fall, in the tiresome passing of seasons,
there are only two cicadas left
they drone on in an endless drill, a final dance,
each an echo of the other.

3

Stella, my mother you sit beside me
small and frail
a bisque doll, head sunken to one side
limbs flopping.

Breathless I hold your hand
certain you *will* break like china
in this silent waiting

fearful and dark I am
a capsized boat in the ocean
flailing with my feet tangled in the sails

waiting for the final coin toss to choose—life or death.

You are my all, my love
playing like a lullaby in my heart
with your small smile
childlike over butterscotch ice cream.

Before you go you must know
I typeset each letter by hand,
print each page I write, sew each book

as shadow and memory
an indelible link
that pens and pencils

an alphabet
for the sentence of the story of my life
that begins once upon a time with you.

My zen is to embrace
what you have done that I choose not to
the zen of cooking and endless cleaning
the zen of loving and endless forgiving
                    you

Queen Mother
with your power brandished through guilt;
guilt—once the alpha and omega of your kingdom
gone away now, an army in defeat.

Mother is a tea rose now—
deaf and fragile
sleeping under the rain.

4

"I *must* talk to you. You *must* answer me!
Read my lips! What do you hear?"
　　"Nothing."
"What does nothing sound like?"
　　"The ocean."
"See Mom. Yes, you can hear!"
　　"No. I cannot hear, but I remember."

5

After years I learn to write daily messages to Stella on a white board,
"Mom it must be hard for you to struggle to hear Dad and me.
Are you angry that you cannot hear?"
　　Stella gazes into the sky, "Lips that were once for kissing
　　now talk to me in little mumbles.
　　I pick and choose like the flowers I like.
　　When your father tells me what to do, I do not hear;
　　besides when I go Home
　　there will be such singing in your brain you don't need ears."

6

"Are you getting ready now for your big adventure Home, Stella?"
　　After some minutes of staring into the sky
　　Stella, *estrella*, a star looking through a black hole asks,
　　"What journey is that?"

"You have been talking about your big adventure—
going Home to be with Jesus and your mother, Mary,
your sisters and brothers. You will see your father there for the first time."
　　Looking at her watch, "Yes, Yes I remember now.
　　It's time. Let's go already. When can we get this going already?"

"I cannot go with you. Chester cannot go with you.
We will be fine here after you go.
This is a big journey that you will take by yourself."

"OK. I will go tonight, but I need my lipstick and a car."

7
For years after therapy
        fall after fall
a slumping rag doll in decrescendo

like the constant chatter of girly gossip
a walker—now her new best friend
the support her Prince husband cannot be.

Screaming
I am running to catch her as she falls
        like a star I cannot reach,
"Mom, use your walker!"
        "I do; it's always waiting for me right there
        in the corner; if I ever think I need it."

8
Strokes and 10 years of dementia have
eased her pain, with a toll
        her hearing and memories, were riches

plundered in a bargain with death
like a barter made with gypsies
        nothing gained without something given.

Stella is our pretty child now
with diapers, bibs and giggles;
we write on a whiteboard to talk to her daily.

She glides
    slides
like a slinky out of her wheel chair,

"Mom where are you going? You are falling!"
    Looking up she giggles,
    "Whoopsie!"

Yelling on the white board,
"Mom, you can't walk! You fall when you walk!"
    She asks, "Every time?"

I swoop down again to write,
like crows intense on carrion
scribbling wildly
"Yes. Every time. You are making me crazy!"
    "Well then lookin' at you girl; that crazy
    must have lasted for quite some time now."

Back to the board,
"Stay in your wheelchair so you don't fall."
    She explains, "I just needed a little more space,
    but my wings got stuck."

9
After a bad day at the office I seek out my old friend,
"Mom, life is not easy for independent women.
If I were a boy I'd be like Chopin.

Delicate. Talented. Famous. Lauded. Applauded
for one beautiful special talent
with a lover to cherish and take care of me;
protect me from the vulgar masses."
    Stella points to her wheelchair, "If I were a boy
    I'd be a wrestler. So I could pitch and kick this thing to death."

10

I write, "How are you today, Mom?"
	"I am sad."
"Why Stella?"
	"He didn't kiss me today."

Chester comes near; Stella wants him.
"Stella, tell Chester what you said."
	"I said, Chester, Dear you didn't kiss me today."

He replies, "Yes, I did."
	"I don't remember."
"I'll kiss you again."

They kiss and hold hands on the couch.
Still love birds, embracing, cooing;
after 75 years each remembers how this goes.

Stella touches his arm, takes his hand,
	"Come upstairs with me now, Dear."

Chester with tears,
has become a pearl in an oyster
years spent washed through the sands of elder care

there are no stairs in this third house he built for her;
the stairs were in the white house

in Bon Air
where the air was good
where they made their family.

11

Chester says, "Your mother was up all night
chattering, jibbering and jabbering
from 1 o'clock to 6. I didn't get any sleep."

"What did you two talk about for five hours?"
    "I didn't."
"Did you jabber back?"
    Chester admits, "I pretended
    to be sleeping and I would snore."

    "Then your Mother tells me,
        'Chester, Chester, I know you are not sleeping.
        You do not snore—ever. I know you are awake.
        Why won't you talk to me oh my Darling?'

    Guilt hangs on his shirt like old stains;
    Chester staggers on his cane, "I am so tired of it all."
    Barabas in the salt mines,
    living from rote memory; eyes closed, laboring on.

12
Scribbling on the board
I need my friend after a day at the office,
"I need a new country, Mom. Some place other than this place."
    Stella asks, "How will you know you have found that place
    and that you have finally arrived there?"

"Everyone will have an insatiable appetite for my ideas
and act on them as if they were the Word of God.
Without committees. Without consensus.

Without meetings. Without debate.
I just want my word to be heeded
like the Word of God for once in my life!"

    Stella speaks out, "That place will certainly make God tired.
    And besides no one does what God says either.
    Well not unless you make it a holiday with pretty food and presents."

13

After years of dementia,
like the Wisla River that traces past Krakow to Warszawa,
Stella reverts to her first language.
I write in Polish to talk to her now.

"Dzien dobry Matka. Jak sie pani ma? Co pani robi?"
"How are you today, Mom? What are you doing?"
    "I'm OK. What are you doing?"
"I'm making preparations. Christmas is coming soon."

    Stella, says, "Me too. I'm preparing for Jesus too.
    I've been preparing for some time."

"Yes Mom, everyone has wished you a good journey.
We will all be okay when you go."

    "Yes, I've been getting ready for the trip.
    My lipstick is packed and all is in order.
    I am ready to visit Jesus. He isn't ready for me yet though.
    He wasn't home when I knocked on the door last night."

14

Stella goes on an outing for Mother's Day
coiffed, with a pink manicure, and pretty clothes
she takes her place at my table
our Queen Mother raw from time and diapers.

    She looks at a high school picture of me.
    A gleam of recognition
    like the sparkle of polished silver
    flashes in her eyes, *"That was my little girl! That was my little girl!"*

I scribble, "That is *me* Mom, a long time ago. Time makes us all old."
    "And fat," she offers.

"Yes and that too."
    "It's made you so old and fat I didn't know who you were."

"Who do you think I am?"
    "That lady who comes to the house,
    cooks, cleans and does dishes every day.
    I didn't know that was my daughter.
    I'm sorry."

"Yes, I am sorry too."

15
Stella calls me "Lettuce" now.
I write, "In two weeks you will be 95 years old
and married to Chester for 75 years.
Do you remember back to June 12, 1937?"
    Stella stares at the words and shrugs her shoulders.

"What do you have to say about your 75th wedding anniversary?
What do you have to say about that?!"
    Stella's fingers search for words
    as if fumbling through a new purse for keys,
    "It is the kind of celebration
    when you should just go underground and keep quiet."

16
Chester's Song

"September is my favorite time
this time of year
the fog in the mornings

crisp like apples bright with the dew
clear days   with the sun
not too hot."
"You know your mother is a poem to me.

Each morning, all day, all night
I attend to her, seeking just the right words to say."

Still she sits there just the same—an empty page.

He rewrites the poem everyday
changing the verses
seeking a rhyme or some rhythm
to bring the dance back

kindle some memory
to flash a fire in her
grateful for one perfect moment—
when she remembers his name.

SHADOWS ON THE BED

Months after her passing Chester admits,
"How I do miss caring for her."

Grief lingers
like an unending chest cold
erupting in coughs and spasms
in fits   moving to that moment of truth
of life or death
when a fever breaks—

     loving was better then
     with the struggle of caring for her spent body
     when she was there
     not knowing who he was
     kissing her small hands and sunken cheeks

     than loving is now
     in these black days and nights
     pining for her in the silence
     of her shadow there on the bed beside his.

IN THE FERN GLADE

The wind that breaks these tall and mighty
trees and cracks them
with their broken limbs
whining against the pressure of time—

this is the same wind
that moves me.

Anchor me in this storm
let me learn
to move like the ferns
in the glade
    gently
        gliding
            calmly

a shadow on the wave
of what is unseen and unknown
    easily
        riding
            waiting

for wings on the flight of death
    in ease
        Joy
            and glory.

5

It is a natural thing to talk sparingly.
Surely this is right—because even

the great wind and lashing rain
do not go on forever.

AT CHAZY LANDING

The orchards roll thick into the bay at Chazy, birds pelting new fruit.
Dairy farms roll herds of Holsteins
into the weathered leagues of Lake Champlain.

There is new hemlock, cedar and birch here;
vegetation is dense, more than a Cape Cod memory where winds
harsh and endless, have knurled the scrub pine, blowing soil away.

Architecture here is a simple poor, no handsome cedar shake salt boxes.
A pre-dawn mist scents the shacks in July; jasmine fills the air
as a familiar lapping erodes the shoreline.

Boats bob above anchor, endlessly without sails or power. Across the way,
Vermont's Green Mountains curl down to the sea leveling a broad plateau,
beneath the rain it is cold in July.

Nearby the Adirondacks cool the heat of harried New Yorkers
escaped like prisoners from the lower Hudson Valley.
At Lake Placid they rediscover their smallness dwarfed by Mt. Marcy.

This is the home of paper, wood and pulp. The Georgia Pacific story. The
"Growth Company" which plants itself in Plattsburgh;
Burlington Papers lies eastward conserving the forest for its own.

At Rouses Point, the Richelieu River empties into Champlain.
Isle La Motte anchors itself and floats beside Grande Isle with St. Albans Bay,
on the eastern shore where Vermont erodes.

The farmlands here are drizzled with apples and honey
as apiaries dot the rims of orchards. The growing season is short;
corn has barely broken ground by July.

The *Press Republican* in Plattsburgh tells everything you need to know
for a simple life here—an old truck, chickens, the birds and the bees,
love at night, and babies bouncing on your knees.

STORM AT CIBOLA VISTA

From the stucco veranda, I take in this big land under an Arizona sun.
I trail through the valley awed by the vastness of the open sky

in the grey-green speckled valley still dotted with horses and cattle,
in these last serene moments before housing developments swallow
the desert skyline like quicksand.

The valley before me ranges up to the mountain slopes that curve
northwest to canyons. Sparse growth dots the desert floor.

Memorial cairns mark where souls of the dead leave the barren landscape,
by accident.

Trails lead up to black, craggy hills, carved and cracked, zigzagging
across ridges; here manzanita gives way to fabled saguaro.

Above the slopes, young jagged mountain ridges sculpt shapes
from a turquoise sky. Here the sun is relentless, brazen and mean,

like a rustler that won't quit, a headache yielding no peace
or bargain for relief.

Beyond my porch, I watch a small herd of horses in the corral.
They have become mine from all these days of caring for them.

Shifting clouds cast a dull shade over the corral. All living things
yearn for the lullaby of night when winds waft the perfume
of purple sage running wild down the canyons.

Beyond this expanse, far out in the valley speckled by shacks and livestock,
the hope of rain rides in on the wind and dust.

Flares of heat lightning sweep across the dark horizon grayed by a full moon.
Horses, snorting and heaving, are restless.

July storms sweep the desert floor seared like burning branding irons
brown in this dry ranch country.

Clouds sailing over Lake Pleasant are clustering and darkening to form an
angry purple mass, galloping above the mountains

in sheets of lightning and a great cascade of rain. The deep rumble of thunder
shocks the hot air before dawn. The horses are leaping.

Dawn is shadowed by this grey storm now escalating to a panorama of
purple over the leagues of Lake Pleasant to the lofty peaks above,

where ancient Anasasi petroglyphs tell Indian stories of hunting and wonder.
For eons it has been the same;

all waiting for the roar of wild water rushing through the washes—
even the cactus are dancing.

After the storm, the sky turns rose and the distant range lightens.
Daylight rages in again like a stallion crossing the blazing sun,
hot and bothered.

SINGING OF FRUIT

Spring

Snows in the highlands
clinging to rocks there. Waiting
to race the run off.

Sap rises gently
in the beech. It is the tree
still trying to find the circle of itself.

Gifts lie in the letting go
without fear or care.
Sheep shearing in March.

March night down by the river.
A cricket rubs her legs
ready for sound.

Night vigil. April frost
in the quaking orchard.
A cold fear blossoms.

Along the dank riverbank
a fern kingdom spawns.
Fiddleheads in spring!

Cherry blossoms in rows.
Spring rises on fragrant wings
singing of fruit.

Summary

Summer

Row turns upon row. Teams of draught
horses rut the fields.
    Seed spirits rise in the air.

        Hot July. Fireflies caught,
        dance in a jar.
           Their cries capture the night.

    Fields growing dream green.
    Heavy laden stalks bear rye.
        light seeps from the moon.

August smells rush forth
piercing the nose while flies buzz.
    Silage fermenting.

      Owls roost. Hungry to learn about
      mice. Their small brown cries
        howl in the wind.

Fall

Cottonwoods willow
yielding to the wind they bend
    forgiving each storm.

       Separate oak limbs
       even touch and bend together
          to weather a storm.

              Joy is not in the walking
              but awakening
                  in the silence there.

       Crisp nights. Stars glitter
       in sky the color of coal.
          Freezing leaves falling.

Winter

A stand of pines crosses the ridge.
Boughs in the wind
      hang firm. Evergreen.

                Snow crusts the feed trough
                lone pony in the pasture
                      the earth warms her feet.

      Princess pine fully green
      above the forest floor
          white fog winds dancing.

                    Sparrows with cold tiny hearts;
                    pepper tracks in snow.
                        Grace just passed by.

          On frozen pastures
          nothing tells it's Christmas
              only the stable glowing.

                  Rain falls on crusted
                  snow. By degrees
                      the ice begins to know itself.

As Spirit moves loving hearts
angels work the night—
      fires dance on stars.

ON THE TIMBERLINE

It is risky to be here
a part of this history with you,
at the reservoir, on the lee shore
softwoods lumber easily
and poised white pines
have been timbered with hacks on the logging line.

I've found you down
a slender one
needles crisp and fragrant.
Your sap once warm and on the rise
now spills, oozing in the March moon.
I ease the quiet bark from around you.
It is brittle,
circled with the age of repetition;
under the bark, your blond center
lies open and silent.

I kneel among the ants and dried leaves
curling at your feet
nestled under this new weight.
Before going I want to linger; imagine
the rowdy red woodpecker at your heights
and the fluid music of pines breathing in the wood.

After the axe, before the fall
I want to hear the giant roar
of your coming in the wind.
And in this new pining
I want to taste the sap of your limbs
and eat the soft wood of life
as you pass by.

IN THE AIR

1

Purple clouds glide over
the last patch of blue at sunset
        a watercolor on the move;
twilight rides over the hill
as three deer are foraging on the browse.

This night, frogs
bury again deep into the mud
April snow just let go
        silence freezes in the pond.

2

All winter
the meanders in the pastures
have been still
their dents and furrows
wrinkle the landscape
        like widows in mourning
        empty and waiting
        to have purpose again.

All at once it comes
        like hatch on a stream
        an avalanche
of hot rain brings the great wash;

the swirl and whirl of rivulets rail
through the meadows connecting pastures.

Where the trout run
the creeks bulge full
there are waves in streams
        striking in their rawness and grace
        choreographed in some phantom harmony
        breathless like dancers
washing over the laurel;

eager to meet
fishermen teeming on the banks
in the gusto of Spring.

3
I have been sitting on stumps
waiting day after day
eyes focused on branches
arms entwined around the oak
ears listening for sap to rise
pacing, watching snow melt
with the memory of the ancients
or a child waiting for gifts on a special day
waiting day after day
a vigil
in endless anticipation of signs
for stands of birch and maple
to pop their buds in red hues
with the sound of trumpets beneath the sky.

Icicles run
      a staccato in the night;
down the ridge, coon hounds
smell it there in the hemlocks
see it there
a shape riding the night.
Fog in the warming;
soon seed spirits will rise in the air.

4
Each twilight
sunset rushes over the bridge
at dusk the sky blushes against the ridge
rose red brushes across hues of robin egg blue
heaven rides on the breeze
oak and maples heave
as the May moon fills the trees with leaves
in the small flowering apple orchard
the fragrance knocks over the bees.

THE GARDENER

1

This is what I remember when January
is deep and February howls—
watering plant beds in June, smells of pine straw
hot and dry under the hemlocks.

Peppermint, fragrant and wild.
Intruding interlopers,
     carpenter bees, ants, grubs
     a raccoon so persistent I have named her,
     tamed her morning and night with food.

This is a lush woodland domain for mountain cats,
coyote, deer; dripping green, growing, untamed;
     no chaparral, mesquite and cholla on the ranch
     in the high desert above Half Moon Bay

     no bougainvillea trained over doorways
     to the streets in Bermuda

     no penny-cress and phottinia hardy in the rain
     at Wroxton Abbey in the Cotswolds in the Oxford years

     no coconut palms outside my veranda, sturdy
     in the hurricane days above Megan's Bay

     no pristine courtyard, bricked, wrought with iron gates
     stuffed with planters under a starless New York City sky

     no endless delicate fragrance of crape myrtle
     at the beach house under the Carolina sun.

Here grows what Wills,
ferns and hemlock in fragile subtle Beauty,
stands of mountain laurel in bloom,
full, tall, and showy but for a moment in June.

2

It is not up to the gardener to say
what will grow here.

I have pulled skunkweed
for eight years and it will not die.

Now, I have come round in the Knowing
to cultivate beds of skunkweed!

I will write articles for horticulture magazines
gardeners from near and far
will visit my mountain cultivars.

I will plant it in mounds,
circle the ponds with it
harvest its prime shoots and make wine

grind it in flour
bake skunkweed bread and muffins
create a new staff of life

brew skunkweed tinctures and essential oils
aromatherapy for a more natural you

dry it and burn it as incense
offerings to the gods

sell seedlings
to convince the world that
what is ugly is worth having.

Then alone in sleep I will conjure
     dreaming of the power of Love
       fondling them until they become roses.

THE ROSE GARDEN

The crocus fold up closed and quiet,
while the daffodils stiff with perfume
spread and pivot to the moon;

in the garden there are red surges below the earth
     swollen like flood waters
     tugging at huge trees
     that have been firm and steady for years;

blue urges to be something else
     prettier, desired, showy
poised and open for the possibilities of night.

I will never be done working in the garden
everything the sun touches
becomes a poem.

MOON WATER

Summer thins, nights cool
zinnias are wild and showy in the garden,
frog songs grate the twilight like
        happy but out of tune lovers;

cicadas break the midnight,
deer watch an evening path to the pond;
the blind dog listens as the acorns fall.

Overhead a hunter's moon
bleaches the stars from the night
pale in a dizzy Indian summer sky;

at the pond, the moon water is still
        barely
                breaking a ripple
as my body dips like a shadow beneath it

Here I am the peaceful Buddah,
under the lily pads in awe, koi hide
        in their fish quiet;
wind flows like incense through the pines.

AT TWILIGHT

1

Storms roll over the ridge
drops thunder down
each frond
      each fern
each and every thing
       quivers in the wind.

At long last yellow trumpet lilies
shimmering iridescent
in the last light of this twilight

stamens and pistils firm and full
shining and gorgeous like
a bunch of beauties on the beach
bold lanky blondes
giggling, shivering and running from the rain.

The storm has moved in
lightening soft and
subtle over the trees
clouds race across the rising moon.

2

In mid-August
air is thick among the corn stalks
it is the corn silk singing on its ear.

A white moon dances
while blue-green cabbage heads
curl up

as the valley fills with fog
all is still
the harvest is sleeping.

3
East of the garden
the grotto is hot and buzzing in the sun
even the peaceful Buddha
is swarmed by a frenzied wave of butterflies
on their way to the lilies;
worker bees drone their magic
inside the pale bells of foxglove

statuary in the pond
is spouting volumes
while hummingbirds
with tiny hearts racing in the heat
are silent and hovering
at the angel's mouth
listening and thirsty.

Hiding deep on the garden floor
ants on parade
carry umbrellas hungry for shade
like mad dogs and Englishmen
under palm fronds in Mombasa.

Deep from the garden floor
the buzzing drones on
frenzied under the pouring sun
while deer discover the raspberries.

EBB TIDE

Sunday morning in the garden.
Rain drips off the zinnias.
Black-eyed Susans are ready to bloom. Maybe today.

The Siamese and Himalayan Blue crouch in the cat mint
patient for the toad that comes up from the pond
      to catch beetles on the balsam.

Salvia blooms short; dwarfed by blue delphiniums.
In mid-July it is time.
It is time to stake the dahlias.

Peppermint and chives
are eager for the salad days.

Time to cut back dried day lilies;
pinch back spent petunias.
Deer have eaten the flowering hostas
      like kids at summer carnival giggling over ice cream.

The garden is a sea of its own
all in an ebb and flow
each a show in its own time.

There is a sudden crest and wave
      a sparrow caught in the ebb tide
feathers fly above the cat mint.

APPALACHIAN HAZE

1

Above the lights and beyond the town
the clouds slice over the pines on the Ridge.
In the heat of June you can see it

an Appalachian haze
hangs heavy thick and blue
gliding through the spaces between the boughs
        connecting worlds like smoke in the air.

The pines are in head
new growth tips the boughs
        in yellow, spring green, new green

cones of all shapes flop to the floor
without a sound
the smell of spruce, fir and balsam all around

waves of pollen ride this wind
cover me tip to toe
        I germinate, merge into new worlds

by twilight I have become a tree
one limb cracks, splinters me into the night
mistletoe is nesting in the silver birch.

2

Two downy woodpeckers
jockey for space in the dead maple
squeaking in a frenzy
chitter chitter twitter twitter
        out on a limb
over the edge with the heat.

Heat has everything crazy
yellow jackets buzzing in the bee balm
beetles dizzy chewing up the zinnias

all in a dither
cats in the birdbath feisty for a fight
splash at the thirsty finches

monarchs in the butterfly bush
hummingbirds darting undaunted
in the foxglove and the hollyhocks

dragon flies bank and dart at the snapdragons
        tap flap and zap
herbs gone to flower; flowers gone to seed
blossoms of color teaming without a weed

the garden with flowers to the gills
tadpoles, frogs, and goldfish blooming in the pond

summer hums with a bountiful heart
a tune of long nights under the moon
keeps fireflies dancing.

3
Like Alice in Wonderland
pruning on my knees
shrinking deeper into the garden

snails wail across the rail
butterflies caught in my hair
hummingbirds at my throat
bees pollinating my ear
        it's a zoo in here!
worms snake across my toes
overturned in this kingdom
were everything grows.

4
Zinnias, summer beauties
on tall legs
you bloom outrageous
showy and painted, bountiful
        like cabaret can can girls.

Like you, we are made
to dance in our place
to kindle Beauty
to add Joy to our show
to walk in Light
knowing this now—is Heaven
and all is holy.

We are children like fireflies
caught in glass jars
each our own bright star.

HARVESTING SEEDPODS

In October the garden is all but spent
here you cannot keep them with you
beauties of the blooming days; ravishing showy days
fading as the calendar turns.

I harvest the pods
their small seeds stick to my skin
stories collecting
      like moths saved in little boxes
pressed in books and among poems.

In dark December when chill surrounds
and warmth races up the chimney
with the flash of firelight

I will plant my seed pods
nurture them as they shoot up new and green
from the dark earth

these will be my children for years to come
blooms red and yellow, purple and vibrant in the sun
for all years, each, one after one.

6

From
Living with Spirit

He who wants nothing is able to achieve everything
Do not be bound up in yourself.

If you can put yourself aside
then you can do things for the whole world.

A DARK ROARING

All in nature carries Grace;
it is the absence of control
each act and response
a balance of the Divine One

rock, crystal, mineral manifest Grace in patterns
sage colors greenish hues
wet in the rain
with moss and lichens thriving on its energy

on the raging wind,
I embrace this tree
my arms and body wrap it
as if in some dance

here, we are linked to all
that's above and below
from the swaying of our limbs in the sky
an inner trembling pulses
from our limbs to the roots below.

This dance is primal, without music
the course of sap rising in my limbs
drumming along my breasts
through my belly

chi, a power surging
a deep dark roaring of the soul.

FOG

It is a calm morning on the mountain
I move among the fog winds dancing
as dawn rises white above the trees.

Snow has covered all over
      again.
In the stillness you hear
sap rising in the sugar maples.

Over the rise
there are shapes in the fog
moaning,

their songs slide
from the creek and valley floor below
over the Ridge

like water
together we flow gently around
and do no harm.

STONES RISING

for C. Boucher

1

In Spring, the earth gives of itself
opening up new chapters
germinating in the spines of winter
the earth is an open book
marked with ribbons of color.

Blossoming orchards
stripe the hillsides
and maples blush
as sap rises through their veins.

2

We dream in metaphor. Each field
and forest makes a new impression
images not yet pressed before
new pages in this life
different from other lives, other poems,
other pages
illuminated
      from the past
      in a marriage of heaven and hell.

3

Each forest
is a collation of pages
      folded and gathered
      as a signature
a personal history
      her story
of how it has been
to walk this way
engraved in black
and colored with the brush of time.

Lives
like an artist's copper plates
etched with the acid of joy and sorrow
from then, now, and tomorrow

each signature a chapter of the lives
we have known and ones
we know not yet how to remember
as we regress our souls
to kinder, gentler places
connected to all we have been
and we have yet to become.

We gather each section of our lives
sewing signatures
each of us a book in time
bound through and to the ages
a name etched in some corner
among another's hand
the paints and pigments
the strokes and brushes

for this great Love
and each Love thereafter is a tribute
the woman whose face shines no light
     his sweet shadow of delight
will ever be a quiet star spinning in the galaxy.

4
In Spring the harrowed fields
of earth give up
    stones rising
pushing up through the ages
with the stresses and forces of time;

what was solid
gets brittle with wear,
edges soften
under running water
and the heaving, freezing,
thawing, gnawing

        edges wear in the corners
        spines crack
        when the mulling over
        wears thin in the novel of time

        songs, poems, sketches and stories
        a chronology of Spirit
        Imagination, Beauty and Joy.

We are each a book of the Soul
a collection of lives
an epic poem
an endless song of Spirit

half-bound
edges worn and fingered
covered with a great leather
    that never wears thin or crumbles
    never cracks at the spine.

DRUMMING HEART

We ride on the Great Mandala
of fire, wind, earth, water and minerals
drumming through the sky
     a tail of a comet
       in a trail of Light and prayer.

Link us to the universe
that knows no bounds;
link us to the religion
where all people are one;

where every thing is holy;
link us to the time
before these new stars;
link our drumming heart
to the breath you breathe.

THIS SAME MOON

Incense wafts on the night
chimes sway in tune on the breeze;
beyond the orchard
deer hide in the patch
eating my stash of raspberries;
birds echo a final chatter as they roost,
fireflies light the night
like the flight of a million stars.

Remember, wherever you are
under God's great sky
come to know
what you run from,
and to, and why.
My moon is your moon
our Light reflects the sun.

WHISPER OF THE HEALER

1

Clever woman, Ginevee
your face moves out
to where the wind blows;
its wrinkles hold sacred mysteries
older than time.

Your clapping sticks hit your thighs
as your smile dwarfs the moon
you teach us woman
clever woman, shaman woman
body painted in red and yellow ochre
colors old as the Outback
walking with your crystals
healing evil in the darkness

dancing in a frenzy around the fire
in the Dreamtime
painting our stories in the sand
you make us become you
protecting all from the shadow of the *bugeen*.

2

Visiting God on the other side of Utopia
Love makes us what we are called to be
pray to become the Light we have received
and the name we bear
in a world with lights contrary to our own.

We live life to heal with Light
so you may know
the tender touch of God.

3

When the mind is quiet
we move among the aura of all livings things
like the hummingbird
focused and intent
on the Divine nectar
that flows between us.

We see your soul spilling out;
tethered and lost—it's blue;
we gather in
little pieces and bits
to repair and balance
     with a soft touch
Spirit guides smile
and close the holes with Light;
we are tiny wonders
hovering over the whisper of God.

THE RAINS OF ROSH HASHANAH

Purple asters in late September
beyond the rains of Rosh Hashanah
beyond Yom Kippur
beyond the High Holy Days
in the grotto the sun
shines on the face of the peaceful Buddha
a stone cairn poised

in the in between time
into the novena days of October prayers,
gratitude looms
      in a ceaseless mantra
      rising like smoke on the wind
      a sweet incense of desire.

The in between time, after the harvest,
the deer stop and click beyond the orchard
white tails flash and scamper
after eating the last apples
twilight comes quick; sun slips
below the Ridge.

The full moon, a brilliant yellow ochre
rises with a haze and a glow
meditating
like goldenrod swaying in the meadow.
The in between time
finds purple asters in bloom
      delicate stars
      small winks in the darkness
      jumping from shadows in the night
      like the halo of the moon
tiny joys to carry me
in this in between time
when my vibrant hair turns gray
frost covered with the secrets of life.

SILENT BIG THINGS

Falling snow melts over me
like glaciers melting from the Earth's tilting
all in a manner of degrees.
These are the silent big things the universe does.

At the Winter's solstice
the New Age comes sliding in—forever softly;
    after decades of wondering and waiting
Aquarius comes gliding in peace.

Angels are crazy happy, singing
about Jesus and Maitreya coming back
Masters teaching us once more
about unconditional Love for every living thing
    every sentient being.

At this new dawn birds are feasting at the feeders
cats watching and yawning;
chipmunks hunkering down in snow under the wood pile.
In the woodlands here, crows are guarding the fern glade;
the vortex in this sacred space is spinning—forever softly.

        – 12/21/2012

7

Learn to yield and be soft if you want to survive
Learn to bend and you will stand tall.

Learn to empty yourself and be filled by the Tao
Learn the way a valley empties itself into a river.

FROM *THREE MONTHS ON THE MOUNTAIN*

Crossing the summit high in these Appalachians
I am on pilgrimage to connect with the Sacred
     like a Buddhist monk in Nepal
     up the holy mountain
     to the stupa at Kathmandu
where the captive world lightens
where the oaks begin to thin
and rock and hemlock take over.

At this height the world is old
pre-Cambrian, summits worn
going on and on to the sea on a quest of their own
     to flow gently around and do no harm.

This is journey enough to quiet the mind
for union, for one enlightened moment when
     All is One. All is Holy.
I come to find my place in this tree of life
     like Abraham and Mohammed
     onto Mecca for the Hajj;

     to walk into the labyrinth
     step after step, seven paths to another world
     wrapped in a parka, only my face is open to the wind
     covered like women of the
     hijab, niqab, and chador
     eyes exposed, open and hungry for Wisdom.

On this trek, body, mind and soul
collide in a perfect storm
lost and seeking peace
weathering squalls from the North, West and East
passing over Laurel Summit
nothing is crossing the mountain
except this blizzard, driving and endless.

The frozen treescape
      stands
           still.

I take refuge in a hot spring;
lifetimes of fears, judgments, obstacles
boiling up, ready to let go; I melt
into the steam; wicked flakes
pelt my naked skin like acupuncture
      healing in continual prayer and ablution;
      this is my Kumbha Mela like a Hindu on the Ganges
      or Bernadette at Lourdes
come here from lifetimes of wandering
to bathe at the Source on this mountain
flowing in an endless erosion of self
until I become a temple.

                    – 2/15

1
"One who enters must pass through this Gate"
    (*Zohar 1:7b*)
I am baptized in this hot spring
in the mountain world here
    All is One
in kinship, my history,
my feminine power, my Sekinah,
my earth, my moon, my family,
    red, yellow, white
seasons passing in a bond of sameness and of differences;
like a hot moon driving the wind
carrying chipmunks, deer, and bear
out of dens to where Spring is no longer a dream,
but a new idea.

Tall oaks sway with beech, maple, hemlock
an ancient family of trees
different yet the same
together they stand, a community in the wind
wrapped in a warm sky;
the unforgettable moaning you hear
is their moving like ancestors
with limbs shaking
to the sounds of a rocking chair
as they
      rock and wait
      rock and wait
      eager and anxious
moaning for life to rise up
out of their veins

waiting to turn a new leaf
as they move between life and death
      rock and wait
      rock and wait
as everything under the sky
blossoms and dies in its own right time.
We die. We cry. We honor our tribe.

           — 2/25

2

In the torpor and daze of the smoke of a spent winter fire,
I hibernate in this wigwam dome set in a stand of hemlock;

crows crack open the morning
male and female, their raven black cries

in partnership; fluttering in a courting frenzy
in union, a continuation of life,
the force of Hokmah, the holy father
      they *Honor One Another.*

Crows protect, defend and value what they cherish
teach me to create magic in morning prayer

one after two
let the wild things do
what the wild things might
a rampage of fury and creation in flight.

                    – 3/7

3
As twilight sinks into darkness
the spaces of sky between the trees blacken.
I have become a star in the night;
a light beam the moon
casts downward through the pines.
Endless soft March rains
wash my breasts under a crescent moon;
this night I am a ceremony,
a confirmation to
        honor myself
chanting and humming
drumming like a Flicker on an empty tree.

I am responsible
for what I have become on this trek;
a rite of passage, a coming of age
        the Binah
in gratitude for the majesty
of God, in this place, in the energy
of every emerging life
waiting for Spring,
to every sentient being, I sing.

                    – 3/12

4

Five endless days of weather, my refuge now an igloo;
I peer out a small hole to find snow up to the roof!
Breathless in awe

my eyes, large as the moon, track across the forest floor
like owls at twilight
feasting on the inestimable Beauty
        a severe frozen landscape holds.

In silence, without fight
I am trapped in the small space of my self
cornered in my cell waiting for a key
                the Hesed,

in an avalanche of compassion
        I am the hungry child in Sudan,
        the battered women of Darfur with no escape
weeping in the smoke of this sweat lodge
emerging in a dream the color of forgiveness
        Love is the One Divine Power

as I forgive myself, I forgive you
as I love all, I love you.

Snow has given this definition to each branch,
each limb, each bough breaking
        not from one wisp of wind
        not from one flake moving

but under the weight
as God spills out of my eyes
and the moon rolls in.

                — 3/17

5

The shadow of a red-tailed hawk
cuts the dawn in severe circles
after five more days of punishing storms
the door can open and I am out!
     Blushing and shaking
     like a bud breaking
     or Noah waiting for the dove to return,
daylight surrenders; kindness enters;
     the Gevurah
as I bow to the purification of life giving rain
     surrender my will to the
     Will of God
a soft fog rises.

Only small pockets of snow remain;
runs rage ripping into creeks and rivers
a cascade of water
        falls
past cliffs lined with laurel,
paper birch curl and
peel where the river winds;
in thick brown runoff
there is so much water
the trout are choking.

           — 3/22

6

Seek only the Truth
to understand the intelligence of God
     Divine Father, Divine Mother
     male and female, Wisdom energy;
     the unity of all, the Tiferet

to channel the Sacred there are no answers
only questions
	what else is possible
	what can be better than this
letting go of judgments and fears.

In another snow storm I see the whitetail deer
hungry for winter's woody browse
bedding down to wait it out.

$$- \; 3/25$$

7
Be here now
	live in the present moment
witnessing the Nezach, the Divine dominion
God in all creation.

I pack up to end this trek and turn, ready to go
where there is no death; only life.

Releasing all shackles to the past
I allow my fire to burn out
completely to ash
	ash to ash, dust to dust
	drowning embers until the hissing stops.

As I turn to leave,
the Yesod; God connects Spirit
forever to my material world.

Geese and robins return from the South
fine drops of rain are dancing on fern heads,
frogs in a small pond nearby
coax tadpoles to bloom.

The Appalachian Spring
                comes
with or without you
            by degrees
Nature in each sentient being
in rebirth, in its own right time.

Smoke from my final fire
spirals as a gray memory
in ancient Algonquin offerings;

in the orchard down the valley
        the air blossoms
                singing of fruit.

                    – 4/10

About the Author

K ATHLEEN M. SEWALK obtained a bachelor of arts degree in communications and writing from the University of Pittsburgh in 1973. A master's degree in communications management was conferred by Indiana University of Pennsylvania in 1983. Her professional accreditation was earned from the International Association of Business Communicators (IABC) in 1985.

Kate participated in the graduate writing program at Clark University in Worcester, Massachusetts as a teaching assistant in the English Department. She apprenticed and served as a Poet and Artist in the Schools sponsored by the National Endowment for the Arts & Humanities and the Massachusetts and Pennsylvania State Councils on the Arts, 1974-1985. She has held memberships in the Modern Language Association and Poets and Writers Inc. of New York. She has taught creative, technical, and business writing at the University of Pittsburgh and St. Francis University, and she has been a member of the adjunct faculty of the Indiana University of Pennsylvania Fine Arts department. She has conducted poetry writing and book arts workshops for Ethnic Bottle Works and Art Works Johnstown.

Published papers, poetry and documentary appear in *College English, Poemmaking: Poets in Classrooms, Francis on the Spot, Past the Conemaugh Yards, After the Storm, Sleeping Under the Rain, Singing of Fruit, Three Months on the Mountain, Harpsichord, Along the Way, American Dream Women, The Cutting Edge, Heirloom Breads of Eastern Europe, The Vortex and Labyrinth on Laurel Ridge,* and *From the Highlands,* as well as a myriad of small press magazines and chap books which have printed individual poems. Art Works Johnstown hosted the gallery premier of *Edition #19,* her innovative interactive book that spins at eye level as a floating mobile enabling the audience to read the pages and touch the relief hand painted watercolor art as they walk through it.

Her business career spans 40 years in corporate communications management for domestic and global financial firms domiciled in New York.

After residing in the New York City area and unable to see the stars, Kate returned to western Pennsylvania where she maintains a geodesic dome. She honors her stewardship of a sacred vortex and labyrinth on several acres surrounding her woodland studio on Laurel Mountain where she hosts workshops and lives with her pets, deer, crows, family and friends.

Glossary

acid river

created by acid mine drainage from a flow of water that drains from coal stocks, or coal washing and handling facilities, carries an abundance of sulphur or sulfide minerals; it colors river beds and river rock yellow to yellow orange and destroys the ecosystem including fish and wild life which depend on the water source

amber

amber filtered lamps of low wattage are used in photographic print darkrooms because the photo sensitive materials used in printing are usually not sensitive to red or amber (red/orange) light; enable the person printing the photo to see as s/he works

Baptism

ceremony of initiation; mystical experience of death and rebirth ultimately reflected in inner consciousness; baptism by water, fire and holy spirit as found in Judaic, Christian and other worldwide traditions

Binah

the third Sefirah; understanding; corresponds to the principle of the holy mother life form

boney pile

a mound of coal waste, sometimes the size of a large hill; "boney" is the waste itself, also known as "slag;" the pile is also known as a slag heap

chase

in letterpress printing; metal frame which holds the metal type and furniture tightened with quoins; the chase is clamped onto the press for rotary letterpress printing; the chase needs to be secure so that the type does not fall out onto the floor when the ink rollers pass over it

dodge and burn

techniques used during the photographic process when printing a photograph from film; manipulation by the photographer of the exposure of a selected area on the photo; dodging decreases the exposure for areas of the print that the photographer wishes to be lighter; burning increases the exposure to areas of the print that should be darker

drift

a horizontal tunnel driven along the mineral vein or seam of coal; a drift may or may not intersect the ground surface

ems/ens

low-height foundry type that does not receive ink in letterpress printing; needed to print blank spaces; portions of an "em;" an uppercase M is generally cast on a square piece of type, so spacing that's square is called an "em quad;" a space that's half that wide is called an "en quad" because an uppercase N is cast on type of that width

fixer

a mix of chemicals used in the final step in the photographic processing of film on paper; removes unexposed silver halide leaving behind the reduced metallic silver that forms the image, making it insensitive to further action by light; without fixing, the remaining silver halide would quickly darken and cause fogging of the image

furniture

in letterpress printing the low-height pieces of wood or metal added to make up the blank areas of a page; done using a printer's mallet upon the imposing stone where quoins are added between furniture and the metal type block to tighten it into the frame which is placed on the press

Gevurah

fifth Sefirah; corresponds to God's power of purification and revelation; severity; judgment

Hajj

religious pilgrimage to Mecca in the Muslim tradition; required once in a lifetime for those who are able to make the trip

Hesed

the fourth Sefirah corresponds to God's abundant blessings and grace

Hod

the eighth Sefirah, submission and splendor, corresponds to God's glory within creation

Hokmah/Hokumah

the second Sefirah; wisdom; corresponds to the holy father life force

Keter
the first Sefirah, the crown; corresponds to God's Will or desire

Kathmandu
pilgrimage site of Buddhist and Hindu traditions in the Kathmandu Valley of Nepal

Kumbah Mela
in Hindu tradition; pilgrimage for ritual devotion, prayer and bathing in sacred waters; held alternately in the Ganges, Dangam, Yamuna, and Godwari rivers

letterpress
oldest method of commercial printing in which raised letters or block images of metal or wood pick up ink from a roller and transfer it to the paper; preferred for high quality archival printed works on rag content paper (made without acid; tough in strength, holds ink color quality to imprint a page able to endure for centuries); a relief-printing process; preceded modern offset lithography which uses water and ink

Lourdes
in Christian tradition; pilgrimage destination commemorating the appearance of the Blessed Virgin Mary; sacred waters there have been the source of miracles

mine portal
the entrance to the mine at the surface

Netzach/Nezah
the seventh Sefirah; victory; corresponds to the Divine dominion of God within and beyond creation

posterize/posterization
photographic process to create a high-contrast image from a film negative; all tone values of gray to black in the film negative are reduced to a few; used in photography for unique graphic appearance

processing
photographic processing is a chemical means by which light sensitive photographic film and paper is treated after being exposed to light in order to produce a negative or positive image; required in photography before digital technology

Rosh Hashanah
the Jewish New Year; first of the High Holy Days which usually occur in the early autumn; believed to be the anniversary of the creation of Adam and Eve, the first man and woman; realizes mankind's role in a Divine universe

Sacraments
Christian mystical initiation ceremonial rites [baptism, eucharistic communion, confirmation, matrimony, holy orders, holy chrism etc.] which correspond to the Sefirot in the Judaic tradition

Sefirah/Sefirot

gradual emanations of God's presence and power of the Divine that link humans to creation and God; ceremonial initiation rites as in the Kabbalah; knowledge of the holy Sefirot enables the initiate to consciously bind his or her self to God's presence and power

Sekinah

the Divine presence and power which is feminine

slugs

low-height pieces of metal used to separate lines of type in letterpress foundry type composition; a slug equals the width of three lines

signatures

a section or gathering of a book, either in the flat or folded state, to which a signature mark has been assigned; technically, the sets of 4, 8, 16, 32, 64, or 128 printed pages when folded

stupa

mound-like structure containing the ashes of Buddhist monks, used as a place of meditation in holy sites

Tiferet

the sixth Sefirah; beauty; corresponds to the underlying unity of God in creation

vein

a bed of coal usually thick enough to be profitably mined, also called a coal seam

wash

occurs after fixation in photographic processing; washing is important to remove the exhausted chemicals from the emulsion, which cause image deterioration if left in place; brown spots will appear on the image if not given enough time in the wash

Yesod

the ninth Sefirah; foundation; corresponds to God's connecting power between the material and spiritual worlds

Yom Kippur

a Jewish high holy day observed with prayers and repentance; in the tenth month of the Jewish calendar; also known as the Day of Atonement

Index of First Lines